Early Reviews for *Zap The Grandma Gap: Connect To Your Family By Connecting Them To Their Family History*

Lisa Louise Cooke, Host of The Genealogy Gems Podcast:
If you are looking for concrete ideas for sharing your family history and inspiring the next generation, look no further than this book. The personal stories and worthwhile activities make this an enjoyable read, and an ongoing resource to every genealogist. Janet's passion for the power of family history in the lives of today's busy families shines throughout the pages!

James Tanner, Genealogy Author and Blogger:
Zap The Grandma Gap is a heads-up, all-out attack on that greatest of all genealogy problems; passing your family traditions and research on to the next and succeeding generations. Janet Hovorka has provided a book overflowing with valuable ideas and suggestions for involving the "younger" generation in genealogy, perhaps without them even knowing about what you are trying to do. This book succeeds in being both entertaining and informative in a way that makes sense rather than preaches. I found that I could relate to many, if not most, of the examples from the book and would encourage all those "Grandmas" and "Grand-pas" out there, or anyone else for that matter, to take heed and read.

Holly T. Hansen, President Family History Expos Inc.:
This is a winning idea book for bringing families together. There is nothing more exciting to me than spending time with my grandchildren and sharing stories with them. They love it, I love, and their parents love it! Zap The Grandma Gap is not only a good read but a great reference book for creating fun family centered activities that treasures and builds firm family values.

Suzanne Curley, Director, Riverton FamilySearch Library:
Janet has woven together a masterful tapestry of family history threads that will bind your family for eternity. This book is a must-read for everyone who treasures family history and wants to make it come alive for future generations.

Amy Coffin, Genealogy Blogger and Author:
Author Janet Hovorka gets it. She understands the value of family history and its impact on our lives. Genealogy isn't just a hobby. It's a means to uncover the knowledge that can influence who we are and how we comprehend our world. Unfortunately, most people don't discover the joys of family history until much later in life. When our relatives die, we lose their family memories, experiences, recipes and other elements of our heritage. To ensure family history is preserved, we need to pass our knowledge and wisdom on to our children so they can learn to appreciate genealogy.
However, kids have a tendency to run away from whatever mom, dad, grandma and grandpa think is cool. How do we get our broods interested in family history? Fortunately, Janet Hovorka's book comes to the rescue. Zap the Grandma Gap is a handy toolbox brimming with inspiration and ideas for getting the "family" into family history. You'll be grateful for the guidance as well as the casual and supportive way in which it is delivered.

Zap

The Grandma Gap

Power Up Workbook

The Particulars About How To Connect With Your Family By Connecting Them To Their Family History

by Janet Hovorka

Cover and introduction illustration by Bob Bonham

Published by Family ChartMasters
P.O. Box 1080
Pleasant Grove, Utah 84062
www.familychartmasters.com
(801)872-4278

For more information, free downloads and new resources see www.zapthegrandmagap.com

International Standard Book Number: 97 -0-9888548-1-9

Table of Contents

Dedicated to my children,
to the future generations of our family,
and the future generations of your family.

Introduction

Are the youth in your family more attached to their iPod or laptop screen than they are to you? How do you connect to your family members and form the kind of close relationships that will support and strengthen them as they grow into successful and grounded adults? What resources are available to help the youth in your family and set them up for healthy and happy lives?

Meet Super Grandma. Super Grandma wants to help you connect to your family members by connecting them to the super grandmas and super grandpas of your past. Family history connects family members in a way that is personal and unique to your family. It gives youth the power to identify with personal heroes, learn life lessons without having to personally go through them, and gain a wise, broad perspective on life. Teaching your children and grandchildren, nieces and nephews, and even your brothers and sisters about their family history can create strong bonds in your family. The connections to your family's past become a framework to empower your relationships and strengthen their futures.

Super Grandma is here to save the day. She also wants to help you save your family's history. We should involve the next generation in their family history now while older generations are available to help. Records, memories and stories are lost every day when older family members die. We have to bridge the gap together today to preserve our past so that future generations will be able to feel the strength that comes from understanding their history. With a greater awareness of their history, a family can build upon or change generational attitudes and character traits as necessary. Your family will be stronger, healthier and happier when they know where they came from.

If family history seems boring then you are doing it wrong. Your family's history encompasses all sorts of topics; music, language, culture, food, fashion, etc. etc. Find the part that interests your family members and then find out what your ancestors were doing with that aspect of your history. Throughout this workbook you will find lots of ideas. Some may work with your family members' interests and some may not. Some will correlate with what happened to your ancestors and some will not. This workbook will help you figure out what will work with your family to strengthen your bonds with them and preserve your history for future generations.

Brainstorm

Your Family

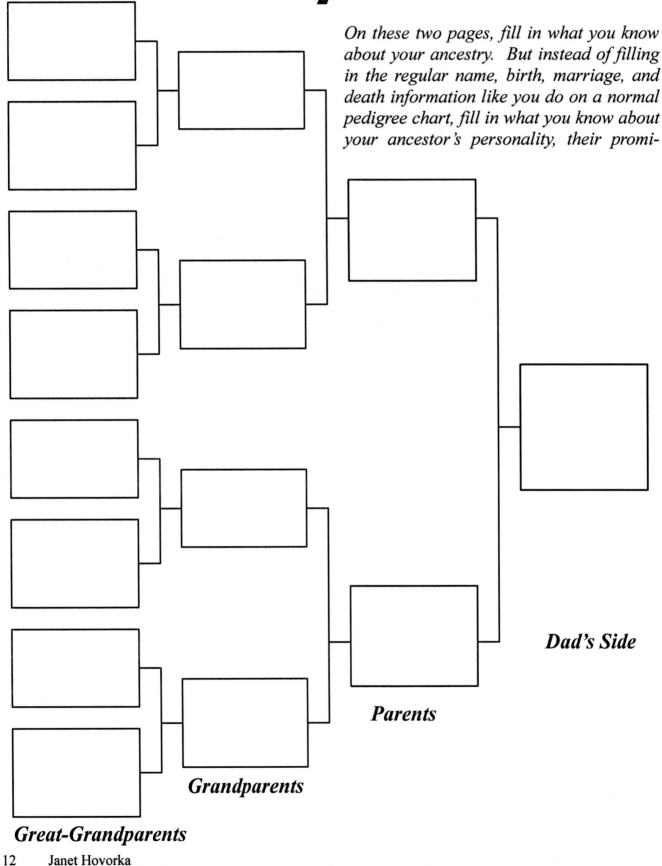

On these two pages, fill in what you know about your ancestry. But instead of filling in the regular name, birth, marriage, and death information like you do on a normal pedigree chart, fill in what you know about your ancestor's personality, their promi-

Dad's Side

Parents

Grandparents

Great-Grandparents

Janet Hovorka

nent characteristics, what they are remembered for, stories you know, etc. If you had to describe your ancestor's character in a couple of words, what would you say? Use these boxes to quantify a few ideas on each ancestor you know.

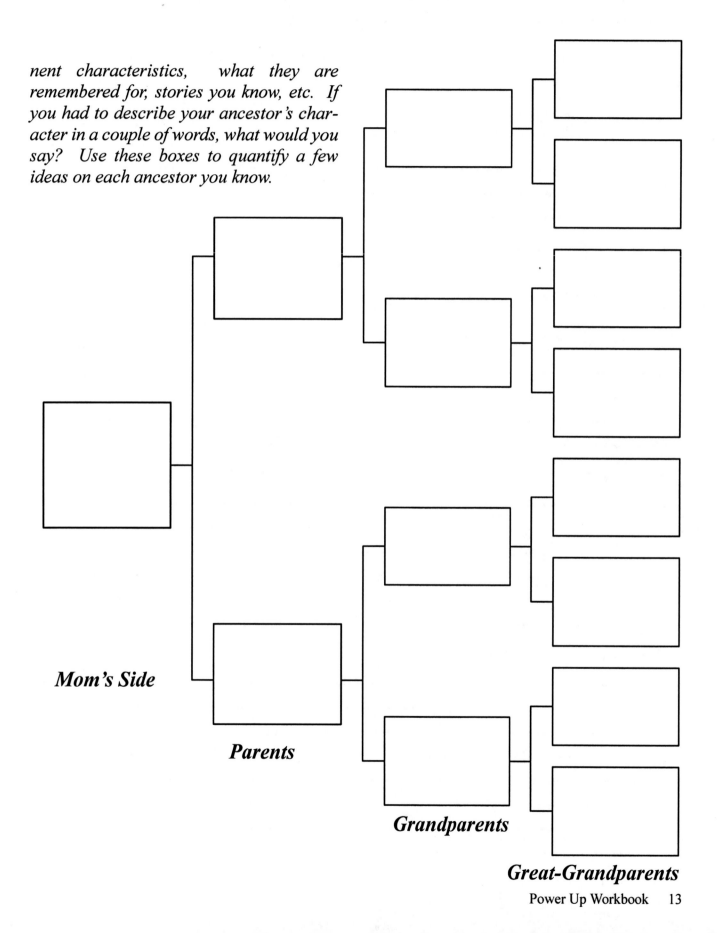

Mom's Side

Parents

Grandparents

Great-Grandparents

Relative Resources

What are the best resources you have for learning about your family's history?

Pictures (look alikes and similar situations)

_____
_____
_____
_____
_____
_____

Favorite Heirlooms

_____
_____
_____
_____
_____
_____

Favorite Recipes

_____
_____
_____
_____
_____

Interesting Documents and Journals

_____
_____
_____
_____
_____
_____
_____

Naming Patterns

_____
_____
_____
_____
_____
_____

Interesting Stories

_____
_____
_____
_____
_____
_____

Living Relatives

_____
_____
_____
_____
_____
_____

Other

_____
_____
_____
_____
_____
_____

Your History

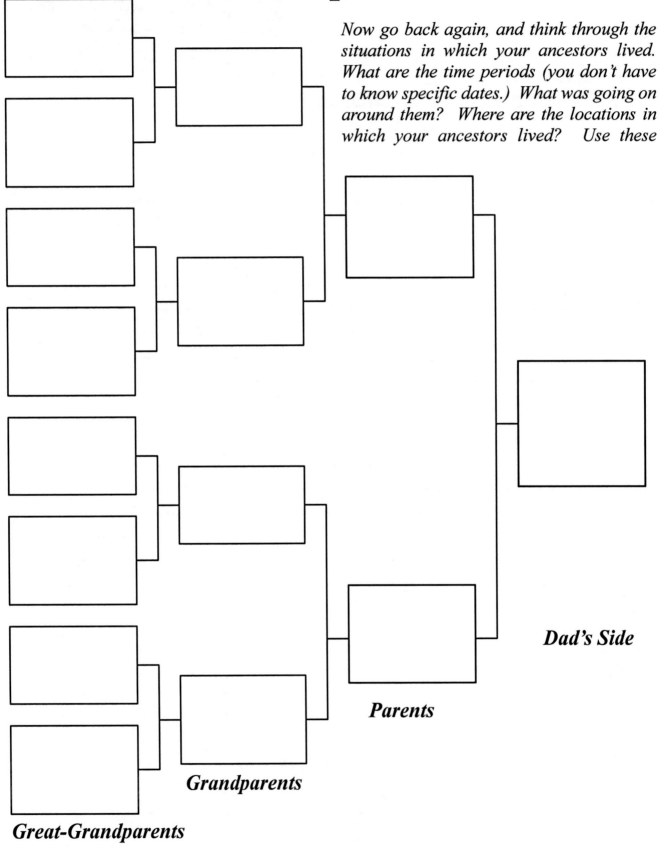

Now go back again, and think through the situations in which your ancestors lived. What are the time periods (you don't have to know specific dates.) What was going on around them? Where are the locations in which your ancestors lived? Use these

Dad's Side

Parents

Grandparents

Great-Grandparents

boxes to brainstorm about the surrounding history in your family's past. What were the cultural forces at work in their lives? Who emigrated? What languages did they speak? Record what you know about the times in which your ancestors lived.

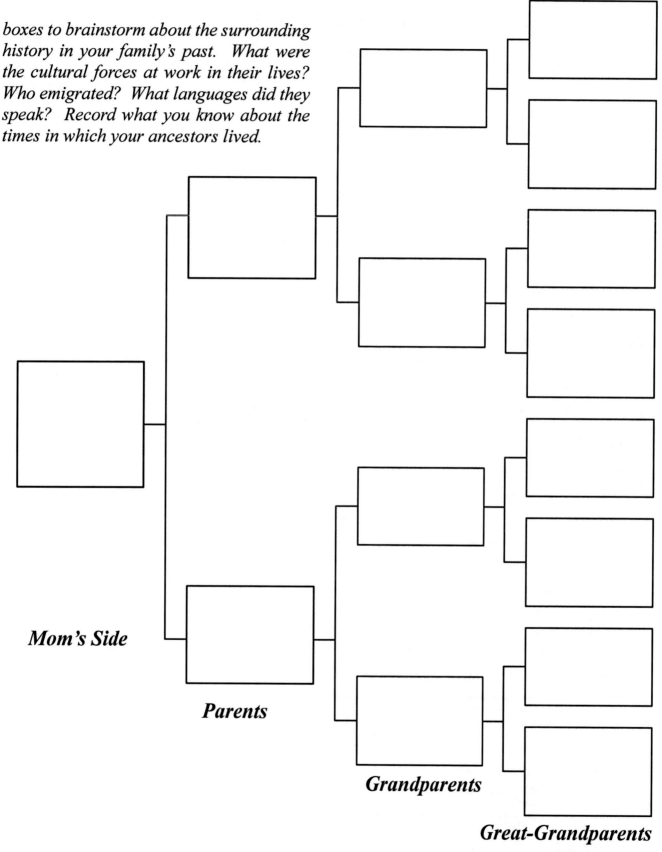

Mom's Side

Parents

Grandparents

Great-Grandparents

Ancestral Assets

What do you know of the life your ancestors lived? What resources do you have to explain what their lives were like?

Culture

_____
_____
_____
_____
_____
_____

Talents

_____
_____
_____
_____
_____
_____

Skills/Work

_____
_____
_____
_____
_____

Music

_____
_____
_____
_____
_____
_____
_____

Traditions

_____
_____
_____
_____
_____
_____

History

_____
_____
_____
_____
_____
_____

Celebrations

_____
_____
_____
_____
_____

Other

_____
_____
_____
_____
_____
_____
_____

General Historical Resources:

Hyper History Online
http://www.hyperhistory.com/online_n2/History_n2/a.html

Timelines of World History
http://en.wikipedia.org/wiki/Timelines_of_world_history

Culture Related Timelines:
http://en.wikipedia.org/wiki/Category:Culture-related_timelines

E History Timeline:
http://ehistory.osu.edu/osu/timeline/timeline.cfm

Your Current Family

Now we begin to engage the next generation in your family with their past. When you bring the family history to the child rather than try to bring the child to family history, the connections will be much easier to forge. Think about the family members you are trying to involve. What interests and hobbies do they have that might tie in to your family history? Do they have any characteristics in common with an ancestor? How do their favorite pursuits fit in to the culture and history around your family's past?

Current Family Member's Name _____
Hobbies and Interests _____

_____

_____

_____

_____

_____

_____

Name _____
Hobbies and Interests _____

_____

_____

_____

_____

_____

_____

_____

Name _____
Hobbies and Interests _____

_____

_____

_____

_____

_____

_____

Name _____

Hobbies and Interests _____

_____

_____

_____

_____

Name _____

Hobbies and Interests _____

_____

_____

_____

_____

_____

_____

_____

_____

_____

_____

Name _____

Hobbies and Interests _____

There is a sweet spot for engaging a child with their family history between the ages of about 7 and 12 years old. In these ages they are old enough to understand time and relationships and they are still young enough to be deeply attached to their family. You can begin to teach the youth in your family about their history in simple ways before these ages and it is never too late to learn about your family history, but when you can catch a child around the pre-teen age, curiosity is likely and the lessons will sink in best.

_____

_____

_____

_____

_____

Now go back through the last eight pages about your family of origin and highlight the places where your ancestral family and your modern family intersect. Those are the areas where you will find natural connections to bridge the generation gap. Look for ideas throughout this book, at http://zapthegrandmagap.com and in Zap The Grandma Gap: Connect To Your Family By Connecting Them To Their Family History for specific ideas and activities on those subjects.

Reflection Questions

*From the first chapter in **Zap the Grandma Gap: Connect With Your Family By Connecting Them To Their Family History**.*

What are some of the issues in your family's past that you would like to see changed in future generations?

_____

_____

What have you done to change those issues?

_____

_____

How can you speak to your family about healthy ways to deal with those issues?

_____

_____

What are the particularly inspiring stories of your ancestry?

_____

_____

Were there hard working immigrants or farmers who built wealth, mothers or fathers who sacrificed for their families, upstanding contributors to the community?

_____

_____

What are the stories you can use to inspire your children and grandchildren?

_____

_____

AHA!

Do you have a family member struggling with extreme challenges right now? Are there any stories in your past of similar trials and uncertainties that may inspire that family member with "I can do this, it is in my DNA?"

_____

_____

_____

_____

Have you ever had any experiences with serendipity while searching out your family history?

_____

_____

_____

_____

WOOSH!

How can you use those serendipity stories to create excitement in your family?

_____

_____

_____

Can you tell the story of your miraculous coincidence in a way that your family will become more curious about the people in your history?

_____

_____

What can you do in general to strengthen the relationships you have with your children? Time spent together? Letters, e-mails, or texts?

_____

_____

How can you be more interested in the hobbies that they have?

_____

_____

How can you trade time spent on their hobby for time spent on your family history?

_____

_____

What hobbies and interests do your family members have now that correlate with the hobbies and interests of your ancestors?

_____

_____

_____

Lessons to Learn

In all families there are hard lessons to learn. If you haven't found a scoundrel yet, you haven't done enough family history, Likewise if you haven't found someone truly inspiring then you haven't done enough family history either. All families have both.

What are the lessons you can learn now from the hindsight your family history gives?

_____
_____
_____
_____

Were there decisions that were later regretted

_____
_____

If there is a history of abuse or neglect, who were the survivors? Who is the hero?

_____
_____
_____

"When you teach about your family's history as lessons to be learned and focus on the resulting triumphs, the problems your family has been through may come to be the most important parts of your family's drama. Those may be the very stories that help and inspire your descendants through the hardest times in their own lives." *(Zap The Grandma Gap: Connect To Your Family By Connecting Them To Their Family History pg. 22)*

Who were the groundbreakers who created the life you have now?

_____
_____
_____
_____

Who were the pivotal figures in your family's past?

_____
_____
_____
_____

Pick a Few Heroes

All heroes have some scoundrel in them, and all scoundrels have some hero in them. Be careful not to glamorize the past beyond what the truth really was. However, one of the best benefits of family history is the perspective it gives over the span of a life and the generosity it teaches when you look at the whole of an individual. With that in mind, pick a few people you really want your family to know well. Figure out who the super heroes are in your family story and make sure the next generation knows them well enough to look up to them and begin to identify with them.

Who are the heroes in your family history?

_____

_____

_____

What are the details that make them inspiring?

_____

_____

_____

_____

Seasons--it may be most effective to choose one person, one family or one branch of your pedigree to focus on for a period of time. If you immerse your family in their history with a laser focus you may hit your target better than if you are trying to cover all your bases at once.

Are there aspects of their stories that are similar to challenges your family face now?

_____

_____

_____

_____

_____

What can you do to introduce your family to these heroes? What resources do you have at your disposal to create interest in their lives now?

_____

_____

_____

_____

_____

_____

Projects

Pictures

Your best assets for engaging the next generation are your pictures. Far and away, the images are what make the past seem real. What you do now with those images will affect the ability of your future family members to relate to their history.

List the places you have pictures stored which need to be organized and made accessible to your family members. What collections do you have and what time periods do they cover?

_____

_____

_____

_____

_____

Organizing boxes of pictures may seem overwhelming.
Just take it one step at a time:

1) Set up a table where the project can stay until completed.
2) Schedule a specific time to work on the project.
3) Organize the pictures being careful to note other pictures around them that might give clues as to who, when and where.
4) Obtain the materials needed to archivally house the pictures. (See page 37)
5) Scan or photograph each picture to create a digital copy for display.
5) Place the pictures in scrapbooks and archival boxes labeling as you go.

Then you can enjoy the benefits:

6) Feel the peace of knowing your heritage is preserved for future generations.
7) Show off your pictures to your family members and use them to illustrate the stories of past generations.
8) Disseminate copies of the important pictures throughout your family.

Scanning Tips:
- Make sure the glass is clean
- Scan two copies of each picture. One large .tiff at 1200+ dpi and one smaller .jpg at 300-600 dpi.
- In your file manager, add information about the people and places in the picture into the metadata.
- Keep copies in at least three places. Two copies on different computer hardware at home (harddrives or computers), and one in a different location.

Your family's historical pictures may not be in your possession. Do any of your living relatives have images of your family's history? Who could you work with to obtain copies of your family's pictures?

_____

_____

_____

_____

_____

Be sensitive to how your relative feels about the family pictures in their possession. These are priceless artifacts and your relative may be concerned about how you treat them. Always show respect for their rights as owner of the images. If your relative is nervous, the least intrusive way to obtain copies of is to just take a picture of the image with your camera or phone. Try to make sure the lighting is right. Be careful of glare from glass. If you show your relative that you treasure these images, you are more likely to end up with someone who is willing to share.

Currently, one of the best ways to obtain digital copies of an image on the go is with a Flip-pal mobile scanner (http://flip-pal.com) It runs on batteries and doesn't need to be attached to a computer. It is quick and can be flipped over and set on top of an image to scan. It also comes with EasyStich software that will combine separate scans of a larger image into one piece.

- Computer screens are 72dpi (dots per inch)
- Consumer inkjet printers @300dpi
- Professional printers 600-1200dpi
- When you enlarge the picture you need more dpi. (Who knows what you might want to do with an image in the future?)
- Doubling the dpi quadruples the size of the file.
- Keep several sizes and formats of your most important pictures.

Visual Displays

What are the classic pictures in your family history. Which images are most iconic of the moments that shaped your family's past?

_____
_____
_____
_____

What images do you have of the most important moments in the lives of your ancestors. Wedding pictures, graduation pictures, professional pictures?

_____
_____
_____
_____
_____

Do you have any images that show off the personality of your ancestors? Are there any pictures of funny moments, or what they did during the day?

_____
_____
_____
_____

Are there any images that relate to an interest or hobby that your family members have now? Are there images of an ancestor at the current ages of your family members? Are there any images that show strong physical characteristics they have in common with your modern family members?

_____
_____
_____
_____
_____
_____

Visually displaying your family history in your home is a way to teach your family members about their past without saying a word.

If you have an heirloom picture, be sure to only display a copy. Light and dust from your home can be very damaging to the photo. Put the original away in an archival scrapbook or box and display a copy where everyone can enjoy it.

The "Photo Detective" Maureen Taylor can help you learn alot from your pictures and even help you identify pictures where information about the picture has been lost. She has written books and articles on how to identify clothing and surroundings. You can access them at http://www.maureentaylor.com. If you have photographs to identify, you may want to hire her for a consultation through her website.

A few picture charts from www.familychartmasters.com

A family history chart with pictures is the ideal family history display because it combines the images with the context of the dates and places in your ancestors' lives. The relationships between the generations are clearly shown so that you can see how the family moved through time and space to get where they are in the current generation.

Visuals of your family history can include:
• Collages
• Maps
• Timelines
• 3D displays
• Working Charts
• Decorative Charts
• Dioramas

Scrapbooks

While your most current pictures are probably digital, you may have many actual hard copy photographs of your family members as well. You should take good care of these photographs as important documents about your family's past. Organizing photos into scrapbooks with archival materials is the best way to store the photos so that your family can access them but not hurt them. Be sure that anything you do to the pictures is completely reversible so that future generations will not have any trouble removing the pictures should the need ever arise.

For digital pictures, it may be easiest to publish them directly into a book. Picture book publishers who make that easy online include:

Shutterfly
http://www.shutterfly.com

SmugMug
http://www.smugmug.com

Blurb
http://www.blurb.com

Snapfish
http://www.snapfish.com

Archival scrapbook materials for preserving physical pictures are listed on pg. 37

On the paper the pictures are attached to, label each image with as much information as you can including:

- Names of people
- Location
- Date
- Circumstances and stories

Uneven Pressure:
One of the most damaging things that can happen to photos is to have pressure put on the photo by surrounding materials. Be careful about what is on the facing page. See pages 168-177 in *Zap The Grandma Gap: Connect To Your Family By Connecting Them To Their Family History* for more information about archival boxes and antique photos such as tintypes or daguerreotypes.

Books

It may seem that writing a book about your ancestors would be a gargantuan task. But there are many easy ways to record your memories and the facts you know about past family members.

A family history may be simply a published oral history interview, captured on audio and then transcribed. Add a few pictures to illustrate the stories and time periods. Who could you interview to find out about past generations in your family?

_____

_____

_____

A family history book that could be very popular with your children and grandchildren might be just one story from your family's past, presented as a children's picture book. You will need a good story and lots of pictures (young people make great illustrators). Stories about something that happened in someone's childhood, immigration stories, or other exciting stories are especially good for this application. What stories in your family's past might work for a picture book?

_____

_____

_____

Small children's books about an ancestor are accessible and digestible for your family members of any age. A short picture book about the life of an ancestor could include one page of pictures, opposite one page about:
- their family of origin
- their youth
- their teen years
- college/career training
- their courtship and marriage
- the years raising a family
- their career
- their hobbies and skills
- their values
- their later years
- the circumstances of their death.

Book Publishing Resources:

Lulu
http://www.lulu.com

Family Heritage Publishers
http://www.familyheritagepublishers.com

Creative Continuum
http://www.creativecontinuum.com

DMT Publishing
http://www.dmtpublishing.com

Organization

Organizational methods are very personal. You need to come up with a system for keeping your family history organized that is easy to you and works the way you think, but you also need to come up with a system that your family members will be able to follow when they inherit your materials. Family History information is commonly organized by family lines, with children's information remaining with their parents until they are married. Each family's information could then be further organized by record type, by event, or by location. Color coding scrapbooks, file folders, etc., is an easy way to distinguish between family lines.

For further ideas that may parallel the way your brain works, take a look at Kimberly Powell's list of articles containing methods for organizing family history at http://genealogy.about.com/od/organization/Organization_for_Genealogists.htm.

How are you going to organize your family's documents?
How can you disseminate physical or digital copies? Who should have copies?

_____

_____

_____

_____

_____

How are you going to organize your family's photographs?
How can you disseminate physical or digital copies? Who should have copies?

_____

_____

_____

_____

_____

What other odd shaped items do you have and where will they be stored?
How can you disseminate physical or digital copies? Who should have copies?

_____

_____

_____

_____

_____

Family History software can help keep your information organized. These computer programs can keep track of documents, conclusions and sources.
Popular softwares include:

RootsMagic:
http://www.rootsmagic.com

Legacy Family Tree:
http://www.legacyfamilytree.com

Family Tree Builder
http://www.myheritage.com

Family Tree Maker
http://www.familytreemaker.com

Reunion
http://www.leisterpro.com

BAZINGA!

How are your digital family files arranged? How are they backed up? Who should receive copies and how often?

_____

_____

_____

_____

_____

_____

_____

_____

Where do you have your family information online?
Where are the passwords kept? Who has access?

_____

_____

_____

_____

_____

_____

_____

Color coded charts also help to show your family members the overall picture and organization of your information. Color coded charts can easily be printed at http://www.familychartmasters.com.

Heirloom Inventory

Like pictures, actual heirlooms from your family history are some of the best tools to engage the curiosity of your family members. In our culture, items that are old have an intrinsic value that most people recognize. It can be very moving to be able to see something that your own ancestors actually owned, something that has withstood the test of time. Heirlooms are most valuable when the story behind them is preserved with the artifact. You can avoid problems now if you begin to plan for where the heirlooms will go in the next generations.

Heirloom Description	Stories attached to the artifact

Along with using your heirlooms to attract the next generation to their history, you will also want to preserve those items for coming generations. These resources sell archival materials that will help you protect your family's artifacts so that your great-great-grandchildren can appreciate your history too.

University Products http://www.universityproducts.com
Hollinger Corporation http://www.hollingercorp.com
Light Impressions http://www.lightimpressionsdirect.com
Gaylord Library Supply Company http://www.gaylord.com
Talas http://www.talasonline.com

Original owner and how they are related	Where the item is now	Who I want to inherit this heirloom

Flowers and Gardens

Most of our ancestors were incredibly connected to the ground they lived on. Whether or not you had farmers who were ancestors, you probably at least have a few who had a kitchen garden or a few pots on a windowsill. Generations of the past used the plants and herbs around them for food and medicine.

Do you have any ancestors who were farmers? Do you know what they planted or what the common crops were around where they lived?

_____

_____

_____

Check the pictures you have of your ancestors. Are there any prominent flowers or plants that you know your ancestors grew?

_____

_____

_____

Be sure to include markers to honor your ancestors. You can purchase markers made from ceramic or metal, or simply label rocks or popsicle sticks.

Gardening Tips and Growing Zones

http://www.usna.usda.gov/Hardzone

http://planthardiness.ars.usda.gov

http://www.garden.org

http://www.bhg.com/gardening

http://www.hgtv.com/gardening

http://www.almanac.com/gardening

http://gardening.about.com

http://www.finegardening.com/

Were any of your grandmothers named after a flower? Do you know what their favorite perfume was or their favorite color?

_____

_____

_____

_____

What fresh vegetables did your ancestors have? What herbs and spices were used in your family's recipes or for healing properties?

_____

_____

_____

Where can you grow plants in and around your home to honor your family history? Do you have a garden plot, planters on a porch, or inside plants?

_____

_____

_____

_____

Resources for Heirloom Plants:

http://rareseeds.com

http://www.heirloomseeds.com

http://www.seedsavers.org

http://www.ohioheirloomseeds.com

http://www.amishlandseeds.com

http://www.grannysheirloomseeds.com

http://www.victoryseeds.com/

Family History Travel

Traveling with children to a family history site is a natural way to bridge the genera-tion gap. It is an opportunity to teach your family about their family history but also gives you time to be together and strengthen family relationships. It is much more than just a family vacation--it is a chance for you to literally share common ground.

Important Tips for Family History Travel With Children:
(Adapted from http://zapthegrandmagap.blogspot.com)

1. *Prepare.* Put together a Google Earth Tour to show them where you are going and who lived there. Google Earth is a valuable tool that keeps their attention.

2. *Focus.* When you try to trace all of the lines in the areas you visit, the kids can get completely overwhelmed. It is good to focus on one line so that they can really come to know those people.

3. *Be flexible.* You can fixate on being disappointed in what doesn't work accord-ing to plan, but it is better to concentrate on how much you do get to experience.

4. *Look for aha moments.* There will be lots of moments when some aspect of your research comes alive. Watch for clues about why your ancestors did what they did.

5. *Sample the local culture.* Try the food, see the sites and be thinking of what your ancestors ate and did.

6. *Schedule down time.* Family history trips are go, go, go, learn, learn, learn. Most family members of all ages will get tired at some point and then they can't absorb as much.

7. *Let the kids pick a few activities.* Most youth can pick some local sites they want to see on any family trip. Again, it is good to have some down time and let them process a little.

8. *Watch for serendipity.* Lots of serendipity opportunities come up when you travel to your ancestor's homes. It makes you feel like they are watching over you.

9. *Read in the car.* When you are traveling—especially by car—you have a captive audience. Use that time to read to your family, show pictures, etc. Refresh their

memories to make these ancestors become more real in the places you are visiting.

10. *Take a chart.* It is useful to have the basic names, dates, and places printed so you can refer to them. And a chart with pictures is even better.

11. *Record the history you are making now.* Don't forget the camera. Let your family members record what they think.

What are some of the nearby family history sites that would make a good day trip or weekend trip?

_____

_____

_____

What are some of the distant locations that would make a good family vacation?

_____

_____

_____

Near your family's residences you may want to visit:
- Cemeteries
- Museums
- Archives and Libraries
- Schools and Churches

Look for the addresses of your ancestors in letters, wills, censuses and journals before you go.

Items to take on a family history trip with the family:
- Copies of journals and stories that tell the history of your family.
- Copies of pictures to illustrate what life was like.
- Travel arrangements such as directions, tickets and reservations
- Still and video cameras to capture the history you are creating now.

Learn how to create virtual Google Earth tours with Lisa Louise Cooke's instructional training discs at http://lisalouisecooke.com/lisa-louise-cookes-store/

Resources for
Traveling with Children:

http://bestfamilytraveladvice.com
http://travelwithkids.about.com
http://www.travelforkids.com
http://family.go.com/travel

Search for articles about children and the destination at regular travel sites such as:

http://www.fodors.com
http://www.tripadvisor.com
http://www.lonelyplanet.com

Antique Games

It is very likely that if your ancestors enjoyed a certain game, you and your children will have fun playing it too. Look through journals, pictures and letters to see if you can find any references to games your ancestors played. Find out what games were popular in the time and location that your ancestor lived.

Button Buzz Saw
String a piece of string through two holes of a large button and tie in a knot to form a circle. Hold one side of the circle in each hand and center the button on the string between your hands. Wind up the button by twirling the string and then bring your hands in and out to make the button spin.

Drop The Handkerchief
The players sit on the ground in a circle facing the center. The person designated as "it" walks around the outside of the circle holding a handkerchief chanting "A tisket, a tasket, a green and yellow basket. I wrote a letter to my love and on the way I dropped it." At some point, the person who is "it" drops the handkerchief behind one of the players and that person grabs the handkerchief and chases the person who is "it" around the circle. If "it" is able to get around the circle and back to the empty seat, then the person carrying the handkerchief now is "it".

Button Button, Who's Got The Button
The players all sit in a circle and the person who is chosen to be "it" holds a button between their palms so that no one else can see it. The person who is "it" then goes to each player and slides their two hands between the hands of each player. At some point the button is left in one of the players hands. A person who is standing out has to figure out which of the people in the group now have the button.

Another version of Button Button is little different: A button is strung on a long piece of string and the string is tied into a large circle. Each player sits in a circle and holds the string in both hands with palms facing down. The person who is "it" stands in the center of the circle. The players move their hands together and apart to touch their own hands together and then touch the hands of the players next to them. As the slide their hands, the button moves around the circle. When "it" guesses who has the button, they trade places with the person holding the button.

Other games the youth in your family might find fun:

- Marbles
- Kick The Can
- Shepherd and Wolf
- Hopscotch
- Cat's Cradle
- Tug of War
- Dominos
- Draughts (Checkers)
- Mancala
- Jacks
- Nine Men's Morris
- Pick Up Sticks
- Quoits (horseshoes or ring toss)
- Yo Yo
- Fox and Geese
- Charades
- Twenty Questions
- Graces
- Corn Cob Darts

Other games that you or your ancestors played as a child:

_____

_____

_____

_____

_____

_____

_____

_____

_____

_____

_____

_____

_____

_____

More Games

Jump Rope Rhymes

Down in the valley where the green grass grows, there sat _____ as pretty as a rose. She sang so high, she sang so sweet, along came _____ and kissed her on the cheek. How many kisses did she get this week? 1, 2, 3 . . . . .

Ladybug, Ladybug, turn around, Ladybug, Ladybug touch the ground.
Ladybug, Ladybug shine your shoes, Ladybug, Ladybug read the news.
Ladybug, ladybug, how old are you? One, two, three, four . . . . .

Miss Mary Mack, Mack, Mack, all dressed in black, black, black
With silver buttons, buttons, buttons, all down her back, back, back.
She asked her mother, mother, mother, for fifteen cents, cents, cents,
To see the elephant, elephant, elephant, jump the fence, fence, fence.
He jumped so high, high, high, he reached the sky, sky, sky,
And he never came back, back, back, till the Fourth of July, lie, lie.

Do you remember your parents or
grandparents teaching you stories or rhymes?

_____
_____
_____
_____
_____
_____
_____
_____
_____
_____
_____
_____
_____
_____

What other songs or rhymes do you remember?

_____

_____

_____

_____

_____

_____

_____

_____

_____

_____

A my name is ALICE and my husband's name is ALBERT,
We live in ALABAMA and we sell APPLES.

B my name is BARBARA and my husband's name is BOBBY,
We live in BERMUDA and we sell BUGS.

C my name is CAROL and my husbands name is CARL,
We live in COLORADO and we sell CRABS.

D my name is DORIS and my husband's name is DAVID
We live in DORCHESTER and we sell DOLLS

Cinderella dressed in yellow
went downstair to kiss a fellow.
Made a mistake
kissed a snake.
How many doctors did it take?

Eeny, meeny miney mo,
Catch a tiger by the toe.
If it hollers, let it go.
My mother says to pick the very best
one and you are it.

Social Networking

You may be connected to your family members through social networking sites but did you know that you can use these applications to teach your family about family history? You just need to use them in a genealogical way. Here are some ideas to help you teach your family members about their past through the tools of the present.

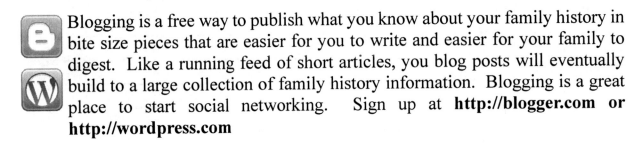

Blogging is a free way to publish what you know about your family history in bite size pieces that are easier for you to write and easier for your family to digest. Like a running feed of short articles, you blog posts will eventually build to a large collection of family history information. Blogging is a great place to start social networking. Sign up at **http://blogger.com or http://wordpress.com**

Facebook is currently the most popular site for checking in with your family and friends. Many people check Facebook daily. Create a page for your ancestor or family line. Post lots of pictures in family history picture albums. Sign up at **http://www.facebook.com**

Twitter is a social networking tool that keeps your posts to 140 characters but you can still teach others a lot about your family history. Create a twitter feed for an ancestor or a family line and post what you know. Sign up at **http://www.twitter.com**

YouTube is a powerful tool because short modern attention spans respond well to quick videos. You can easily create videos of your family history using Camtasia software (http://www.techsmith.com/) Create a channel for your family history at **http://www.youtube.com**

Pinterest is a bookmarking system that helps you collect ideas from all over the web. Pin webpages into collections about each of your family lines. Your pins show up in the feeds of people who follow you. Sign up at **http://www.pinterest.com**

Google+ is a place to post pictures, websites, and status updates about your family history. Like Facebook, many people check their Google+ feed daily. Organize your family and friends into "circles" for separate posts. Your Google+ account is tied into your google account at **http://www.google.com**

Skype is a tool for video chat across the internet. Great for telling stories to grandchildren or doing personal history interviews. **http://www.skype.com**

Which of your family members are on which social networking sites?

Name	Social Sites

How can you use the social networking sites you already access in a more genealogical way? How can you use them for your own research more effectively? And how can you use them to share your findings with your family more efficiently?

_____

_____

_____

_____

_____

_____

What social networking sites do your family members check every day? Which are the social networking sites with the most reach in your family?

_____

_____

_____

_____

_____

More Social Networking

Most Important Social Networking Hints:

- *Keep it short.* Remember they are only a click away from looking elsewhere.
- *Keep it graphical.* The key to keeping their attention online is to fill your social networking with images.
- *Keep it interconnected.* Start with a blog post and then link to it on Google+, Facebook and Twitter. Use http://www.hootsuite.com to keep them all connected.
- *Connect with the genealogy community while you are connecting with your family.* You'll learn lots from what the experts are saying.

What are some of the short, engaging stories you could write about in your social networking? What are some themes upon which you could base a series of posts?

_____

_____

_____

_____

Social Networking Resources:

http://www.blogginggenealogy.com

http://www.geneabloggers.com

http://www.genealogygems.com

http://twitter.com/familysearch

http://twitter.com/ancestrydotcom

http://twitter.com/myheritage

Zap The Grandma Gap Resources:
http://www.zapthegrandmagap.blogspot.com

http://www.facebook.com/zapthegrandmagap

http://www.twitter.com/zapgrandmagap

http://www.youtube.com/janethovorka

http://pinterest.com/janethovorka/youth-and-genealogy/

https://plus.google.com/u/0/10211054088136 5960610

Templates

Calendar

Create a calendar with family history dates and anniversaries.

Together with your children or grandchildren, create a calendar for your family. This can be a great activity for teaching younger children about the days of the week and the calendar while you are teaching them about their family history.

1) Make 12 copies of the opposite page
2) Let the children decorate the pages with the names of the months, and the dates for the coming year.
3) Add any important dates or meaningful memories for your family.
4) Decorate the chart with copies of pictures or drawings of your family members, including ancestors and modern family members.
5) If you decorate the back of each page, you can bind the pages together to display with the back of the previous month above the current month. Or, simply display each page separately at the appropriate time.

Calendar creation resources:

http://www.lulu.com/publish/calendars

http://www.zazzle.com/custom/calendars

http://blog.myheritage.com/2012/03/new-at-myheritage--beautiful-printed-family-calendars-created-in-one-click

http://www.printablecalendar.ca

See also the online photo sharing sites on pg. 32

You can include:
- Birthdays,
- Wedding anniversaries
- Anniversaries of deaths
- Important events in your family's history
- Living relatives' information
- Ancestors' information

You can also include;
- Personality qualities
- Stories
- Sayings and mottos
- Scriptures
- Copies of historical pictures
- Copies of modern pictures
- Drawings
- Images of documents
- Photos of heirlooms

Sunday	Monday	Tuesday	Wednesday	Thursday	Friday	Saturday

Indexing Chart

Use this chart to help everyone stay focused on the goal when working on a family indexing project. Create milestones to celebrate your accomplishments.

Goal: Reward:										
Goal: Reward:										
Goal: Reward:										
Goal: Reward:										

Pedigree Charts

Fill out the pedigree charts on the following pages together. Use the activity to teach not only dates and places but personality qualities and stories. Show pictures of each ancestor and talk about memories. The pedigree charts here can be used as one activity or as the framework for a series of activities, each focused on a different ancestor. Use the chart as a starting point for more research and more curiosity.

You could fill in the chart with:

- Names of the child's ancestors
- Birth date and/or place
- Marriage date and/or place
- Death date and/or place
- Small pictures
- Personality qualities
- Values
- Lessons learned
- Favorites
- Memories
- Story prompts
- Emmigration information
- Fill in the blank spots of research needed

For color copies of the following pages go to:
http://zapthegrandmagap.com/downloads

For a larger chart, and other chart options go to:
http://zapthegrandmagap.com/charts

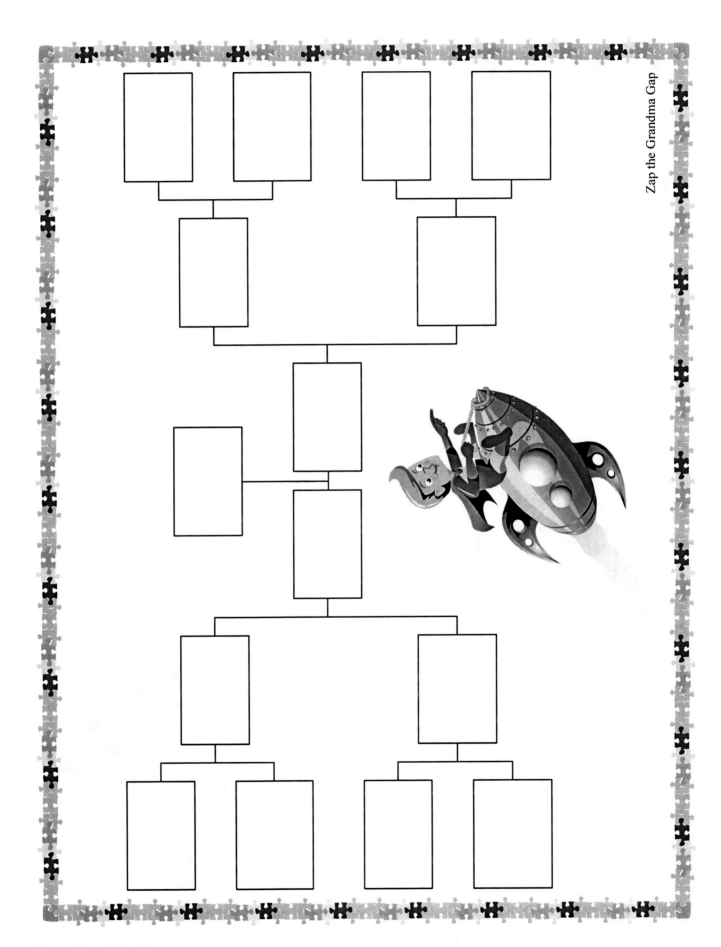

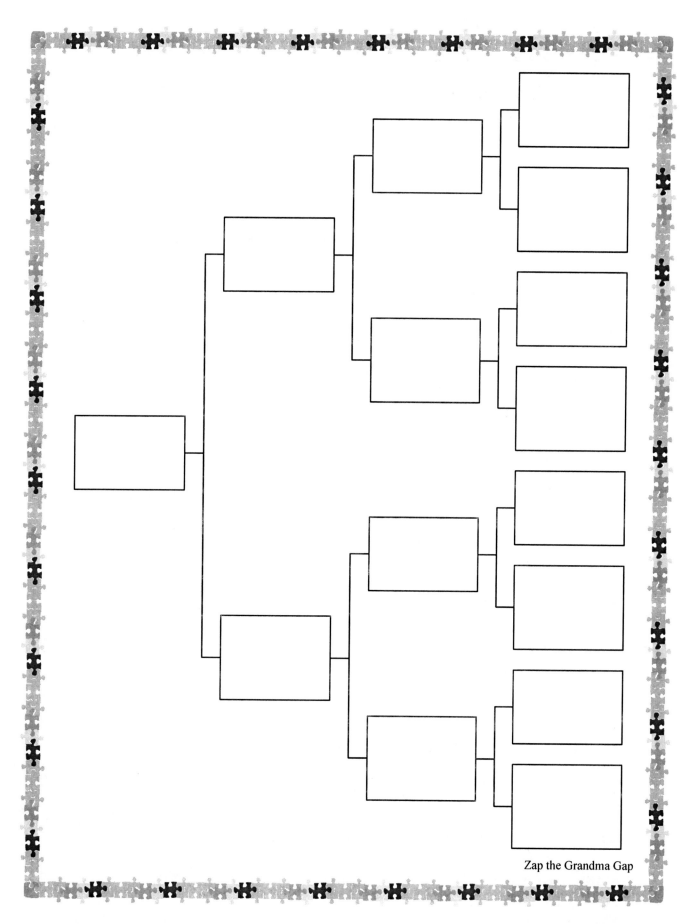

Zap the Grandma Gap

Paper Doll Family

Make and decorate a paper doll chain or use these figures as starting places to create your own paper doll family. Use the dolls to tell stories from your own family's history.

Online resources for paper dolls:

http://store.doverpublications.com/by-subject-paper-dolls.html

http://heritagepaperdolls.blogspot.com

http://paperdollcreations.com/1865family.html and
http://paperdollcreations.com/1860family.html

http://www.fancyephemera.com/paperdolls.html

http://www.education.com/worksheets/paper-dolls

http://www.ehow.com/how_6738378_make-dollhouse-out-cardboard-box.html

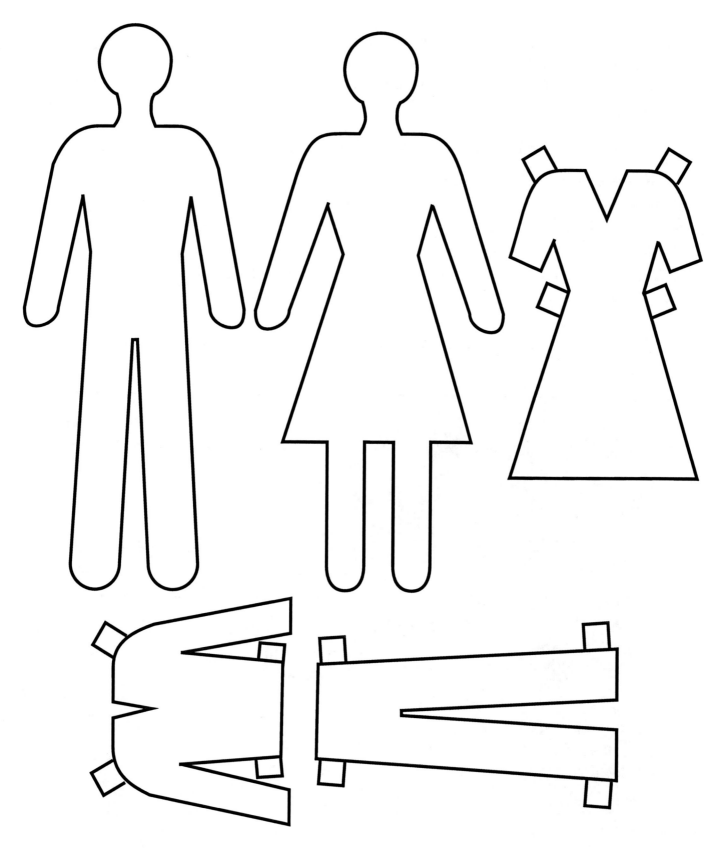

Recipe Cards

As your family eats together, make sure they know where your family history recipes originate. Make an event out of cooking your family history recipes--especially if the instructions are tricky or time intensive. Spend some quality time together while you cook. Talk about where your recipes come from and who the people were who made these recipes before you.

What are your favorite recipes from your father's side of the family?

_____

_____

_____

_____

What are your favorite recipes from your mother's side of the family?

_____

_____

_____

_____

Directions for recipe cards:

Copy the facing page on card-stock paper. Cut out the two cards and fold along the dotted line. Fill out the information on the front about your ancestor who used the recipe and add a photo or have a child draw a picture of the ancestor. Record the ingredients and instructions for the recipe continuing on the back of the card if necessary. Add stories about the ancestor on the other side (inside the fold) and laminate for durability.

What were common ingredients that your ancestors used that are still available to us today? What ingredients are hard to find?

_____

_____

_____

_____

Are there any ethnic trends in your family's traditional foods? Where do they come from?

_____

_____

_____

_____

Family Heritage Recipe

Recipe for:

Prepared by:

Birthdate:

Birthplace:

Photo

Ingredients:

Instructions:

Family Heritage Recipe

Recipe for:

Prepared by:

Birthdate:

Birthplace:

Photo

Ingredients:

Instructions:

Family History Baking

Sugar can make your family history sweeter. If you like to bake, how about creating some family history that will leave everyone with a good taste in their mouth? You can re-create a family home in gingerbread, or make a pedigree chart with sugar cookies. Get the kids involved and make some new memories. Be sure to tell them about who your sugar creations are about as you are working together.

What family gathering could you create a family history sugar creation for? Who could you enlist to help you?

_____

_____

_____

_____

_____

_____

_____

Creating a family history gingerbread house:

1) Secure pictures of the family history home. Get images from every side of the home if possible. http://maps.google.com street view may be able to help.

2) Create a model of the house using posterboard and tape. Assemble the pieces to make sure each of the walls fit together well. Then disassemble the pieces and use them as patterns to cut out the cookies. (You may be tempted to skip this step if the house is fairly simple but don't. It is much easier to correct any problems before the cookies are cut and baked.)

3) Make your favorite gingerbread house dough. Cut out and bake each of the pieces. After baking trim each piece according to the pattern.

4) Assemble the house using royal icing. Decorate it with candies and more frosting.

5) Take pictures and show off your creation to your family. Serve cookies and milk and tell stories about the home and the people who lived there. Point out different rooms or areas of the home where some things happened. Watch the children in your family devour the stories about their family's past.

Resources and recipes for creating gingerbread houses:

http://www.simplyrecipes.com/recipes/how_to_make_a_gingerbread_house

http://www.foodnetwork.com/recipes/gale-gand/gingerbread-use-recipe/index.html

http://www.marthastewart.com/258923/gingerbread-for-gingerbread-house-kit

What family history site or family group could you create out of cookies?

_____

_____

_____

_____

_____

_____

Creating a family history cookie pedigree:

1) Make your favorite sugar cookie recipe. Roll out the dough and cut circles for cookies using a large drinking class. Bake according to directions.

2) On a large piece of cardboard, arrange the cookies according to your family's relationships. Create lines between the families with licorice to show how everyone is related.

3) Decorate each cookie to look like the person using frosting, licorice, mini M&Ms, colored sugar, chocolate sprinkles and other candies.

4) Take pictures. Present at your family get together and enjoy.

5) Upload your pictures to the submit an idea page at http://zapthegrandmagap.com/ideas.html or e-mail us at janet@zapthegrandmagap.com and let us know how your family liked it.

Family History Parties

Everything is more fun when you make a party out of it. From large family reunions to small tea parties with a grandchild, any opportunity to eat some treats and play some games is fun time spent together. Learning about family history while you spend that time together makes the memories even more nourishing to the soul.

The key to making any party special is the planning and the details. Every party has the same basic details and a family history party is no different. Just think about it in a family history way. Get creative about how your family's details can fit into a party theme.

Date and Time _____

Location _____

Pick an ancestor and host a "Guess Who's Coming to Dinner Party", or celebrate an ancestor's birthday or wedding anniversary. Your get together may be a kick off or reward for accomplishing a family history project together. Celebrate one of the holidays your ancestors might have celebrated or put on a family talent show.

Theme _____

_____

Guest List:

RSVP   RSVP

Family Reunion Resources:

http://family-reunion.com

http://www.reunionsmag.com

http://www.bhg.com/health-family/reunions

Music. What music can you use to set the mood and transport your family back in time? What was the genre of the time period you are focused on?

_____

_____

_____

_____

Activities. Choose some games from pages 42-45 or work on a family history project together such as interviewing relatives or creating scrapbook pages about your family. You could watch family movies together or learn about the culture of your ancestors. You can turn any of the activities in this book into a family history party.

_____

_____

_____

_____

_____

_____

Food. What family recipes can be adapted to a party? Will you have a main meal or only munchies and sweets?

Menu   To buy:

_____   _____

_____   _____

_____   _____

_____   _____

_____   _____

_____   _____

_____   _____

_____   _____

_____   _____

_____   _____

_____   _____

_____   _____

More Party Planning

Decorations. Check the visuals and pictures section of this book and *Zap The Grandma Gap: Connect With Your Family By Connecting Them To Their Family History.* Make sure to show off any heirlooms, photos, charts and maps.

_____
_____
_____
_____
_____
_____

Favors: Choose something that the attendees can keep to remind them of what they learned about their family history. Send them home with copies of pictures, books, games or food your ancestors had. Check page 82 for family history gift ideas.

_____
_____
_____
_____
_____

Equipment and supplies needed:

Camera and video recorder

_____   _____
_____   _____
_____   _____
_____   _____
_____   _____
_____   _____
_____   _____
_____   _____

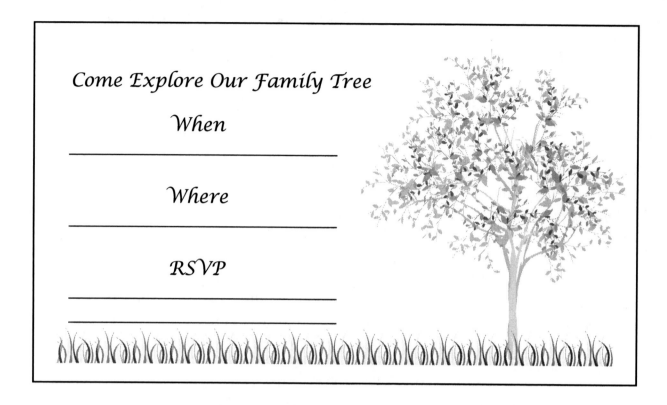

Come Explore Our Family Tree

When

_____

Where

_____

RSVP

_____

_____

For color copies of this page go to: http://zapthegrandmagap.com/downloads

You Are An Important Piece Of Our Puzzle
Won't you join us for a party to learn more about our family?

When

_____

Where

_____

RSVP

_____

_____

Family History Bingo

Bingo can be a fun game for large groups or small groups. Follow these step by step instructions to create a family history bingo game to help your family members learn more about the stories behind their past.

Instructions:

1) Make several copies of the family history bingo card on the facing page. Fill in the blanks on each card with the name and/or pictures of your ancestors and living relatives. Make sure that each card is different.

2) Copy the following pages of bingo cards on cardstock paper and fill out the blanks according to the details in your family. Make as many copies as you need to of the last page and create cards that tell about your family's history. You can create the extra cards with vital statistics, stories, personalities, etc.—anything that teach the players about your family history. You may want to add the correct answers to some of the cards.

3) Cut out the cards. If desired, you can laminate all of the cards for durability.

4) Gather your family for a game of family history bingo. Use small coins for tokens, or use candy such as M&Ms or Skittles to mark the places that are called. Have prizes for the winner such as candy bars with a paper wrapper about their family history, or other small games or dolls that have to do with your family history.
See the incentives on page 97 for ideas on family history coupons or rewards.

5) Family history bingo also makes a great gift for family members who live in different households.

Puzzles can also be great fun for family history learning. You can create a family history puzzle from a pedigree chart or family picture. Resources for creating a family history puzzle include:

http://www.piczzle.com/

http://www.zazzle.com/custom/puzzles

Many craft stores also have simple puzzle making machines.

Family History Bingo

		FREE SPACE		

Who worked at

_____?

(Career)

Which family member has your same color hair?

Who is your Grandmother on your Dad's side?

Who immigrated to the United States?

Who was alive during the first moon landing?

Who was born in the month of

_____?

Who is the youngest person on your bingo card?

Who married in a different country than their birth?

Who lived long enough to see their great-grandchildren?

Who owned a horse?

Who served in the military?

Who lived before the electric light?

Who spoke a language other than English?

Who grew their own food?

Put one token on a parent and another token on their child.

Who first owned a television?

Who was born in
_____ ?
(year)

Who was the first
person born on your
bingo card?

Who was born in
_____ ?
(year)

Who is the oldest
living member of
your family?

Who was born in
_____ ?
(place)

Who is the youngest
member of your
family?

Who was born in
_____ ?
(place)

Who is the oldest
ancestor you knew?

Games to Adapt

Any game can be played in a family history way if you use your creativity.

Many games can be adapted to teach about your family's history. Games such as Trivial Pursuit, Monopoly, Pictionary or Charades can be played with family history questions and locations. You can also play games such as Scrabble or Boggle using only family history names or locations. You may need to give everyone a few minutes to brush up on their family history knowledge, or give them a couple of weeks to prepare.

What are your family's favorite games?

_____

_____

_____

How can you adapt your family's favorite games to teach more about family history?

_____

_____

_____

_____

_____

_____

_____

Jeopardy Labs

http://jeopardylabs.com/
Jeopardy Labs is a website that will let you create an interactive Jeopardy game online that your family can play together. You build and play the game online. It is completely free if you don't mind other people looking at the game you've created. Or for a $20 lifetime membership you can set your game to be private. It might be useful to leave it public where you might pick up a cousin or two.

Scavenger Hunt

For a family history get together, or as a gift, create a scavenger hunt out of your family history documents.

- You can create the hunt to be played at a family history center or library where the participants will have to find the document in the library's collection before they can search out the clues.
- Alternatively, you can make copies of the documents and post them around the building you meet in and provide a map for the family to go find the documents.
- An internet scavenger hunt can even be created with hints on where to find the information around the internet. Just create clues as to where the information might be found, and then provide questions that can be answered in order to win the game.
- A treasure hunt could be a one time event, or a series of questions spread out over time.
- It can cover one person's life, a branch of the family or your whole family tree.
- It could be timed so that the winner is the person who completes it the fastest or you could provide prizes for everyone who completes the hunt.

Write the questions so that your family learns more about how to read and interpret the documents created during your ancestors' lifetime.

Where did Elvis live in 1956?

_____

_____

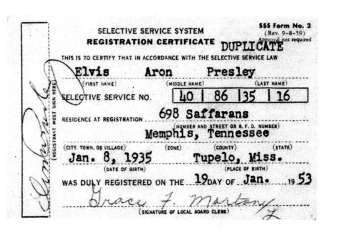

What was Elvis' middle name and when did he register for the Selective Service?

_____

_____

Family Playing Cards

Family playing cards can almost be like flash cards teaching your family about their family history by seeing the images and information over and over again. The learning is easy when you are playing a game.

Match up sets of 2 to play games like Memory, Go Fish, or Old Maid

Create suits of 4 to play Crazy Eights, War or other card games.

Once your cards are completed, you can find all sorts of games to play with them. Rules can be found at http://www.pagat.com and http://en.wikipedia.org/wiki/Card_game

Items that could be included on family history playing cards.
Use these qualities to match up sets of people so that games can be played.

- Pictures
- Names
- Places
- Personality Qualities
- Older and younger pictures
- Relationship to the present day
- Lineage
- Spouses
- Parents and Children

Directions for creating family history playing cards:

1) Plan out the matching sets of two or four ancestors to create the game.

2) Collect the pictures and information necessary to fill out the cards.

3) Copy the templates on the next pages and create a card for each person in the deck. List the matching person on the bottom of each card and the quality that creates the matches on the top.

4) Copy the cards onto cardstock paper and cut out. Keep the back of the cards blank so that competing players can't see which card is which. Laminate and trim cards for durability.

5) Gather your family for a game night or send off to a family member as a gift.

Use this page to organize your ancestors into sets by family group, personality qualities, generation or lineage.

Or create pairs of older and younger cards for the same person, spouses, or parents and children.

Group:	Group:

Group:	Group:

Group:	Group:

Group:	Group:

Group:	Group:

Group:	Group:

Sample Playing Cards

Hard Working

Sarah Shore
born 16 March 1887
Hooper, Utah
Match A. Carpenter, D.
Dana,& E. Snow

Hard Working

Darrell C. Dana
born 14 June 1921
Ogden, Utah
Match A. Carpenter, S.
Shore,& E. Snow

Grandmother

Carolyn Christensen
born 4 April 1949
Lingfield, England
Match current picture to
8th grade picture

Grandmother

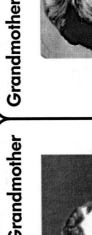

Carolyn Christensen
born 4 April 1949
Lingfield, England
Match 8th grade picture
to current picture

Great-Great-Great-Grandfather

Joseph Hatten Carpenter
born 4 April 1861
Devenport England
Matches: spouse
Matilda Sophia Alder

Great-Great-Grandmother

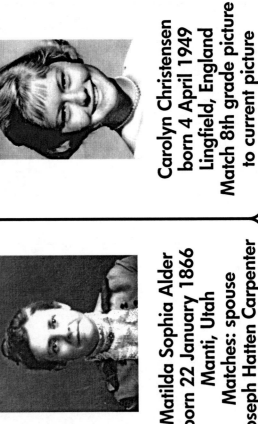

Matilda Sophia Alder
born 22 January 1866
Manti, Utah
Matches: spouse
Joseph Hatten Carpenter

Name _____

Born _____

_____

Matches _____

_____

Name _____

Born _____

_____

Matches _____

_____

Name _____

Born _____

_____

Matches _____

_____

Name _____

Born _____

_____

Matches _____

_____

Name _____

Born _____

_____

Matches _____

_____

Name _____

Born _____

_____

Matches _____

_____

Name _____

Born _____

_____

Matches _____

_____

Name _____

Born _____

_____

Matches _____

_____

Activity Books

A family history activity book can make a great gift or game or favor for a family history event. The youth in your family will enjoy learning about their ancestors as they solve the puzzles and color the pages. You can create the workbook in any regular document program such as Microsoft Word, or if you have the ability, you can create one in a design program such as Photoshop. A hand drawn book could be a real treasure too. You can make copies of the pages and staple them together, or publish it for several members of the family using the book publishing resources on page 33. No matter how you do it, your family history activity book will be a fun way for your family members to learn about your family history.

Pages in an activity book can include:
- Coloring pages (have some of the youth in your family help if you aren't an artist.)
- Dot to Dot
- Mazes
- Crossword puzzles
- Fill in the blanks
- Wordsearch puzzle
- Scrambled words or places
- Matching
- Cryptograms
- Stories (Be sure to tell lots of stories throughout the book.)

Creating an activity book is much easier than it used to be. There are websites that create puzzles automatically from your information. Just type in the answers and questions for each puzzle and with a click of a button your puzzle is created.

http://www.discoveryeducation.com/puzzlemaker

http://www.puzzle-maker.com

http://www.puzzlefast.com

http://jeopardylabs.com

Can you help Joseph Hatten Carpenter sail to Australia?

Created at http://www.discoveryeducation.com/puzzlemaker

Family Ornaments

You can decorate for any holiday that your ancestors celebrated or any holiday that celebrates your ancestors with the ornaments below. Let the youth in your family help attach pictures and fill in the names and information. Trace or copy the ornament onto patterned or metallic paper in the color of the holiday. String with ribbons and hang on any garland, tree or wreath.

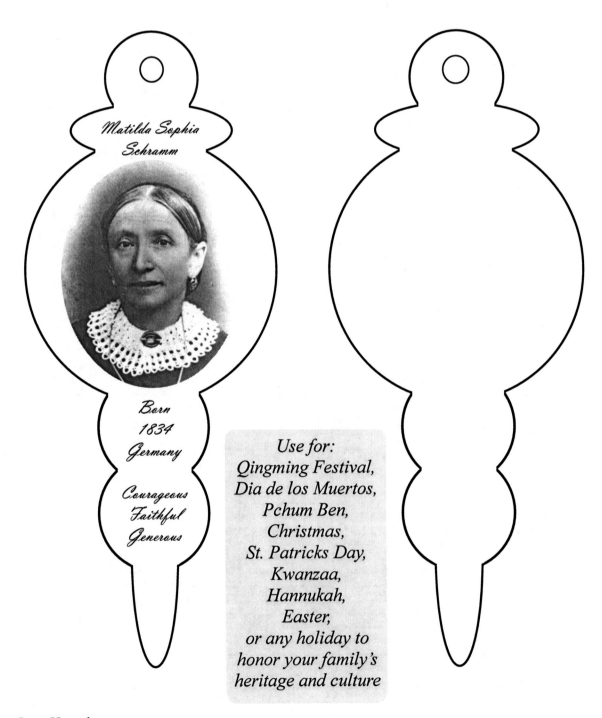

Matilda Sophia
Schramm

Born
1834
Germany

Courageous
Faithful
Generous

Use for:
Qingming Festival,
Dia de los Muertos,
Pchum Ben,
Christmas,
St. Patricks Day,
Kwanzaa,
Hannukah,
Easter,
or any holiday to
honor your family's
heritage and culture

Resources

Family History Gifts

Family history gifts are meaningful because of the effort and thoughtfulness it takes to give one. And the gift can be very important to building the identity and self esteem of the recipient.

Family history gifts are effective because they disseminate the family history throughout the family. They also create a deadline for finishing a family history project. If a gift giving occasion is coming up you might want to put out hints about what you would like to receive. When I was young I always appreciated family history related gift hints from my mother because they were usually inexpensive and I knew she would love the gift. But you can give family history gifts to your family members as well. Any of the projects in this book could be a family history gift. Here are a few more ideas:

- Framed picture(s)
- Heirloom with a story and/or picture
- Google Earth tour
- Collage
- Art piece
- New journal
- Collection of family history recipes
- Time capsule
- Bingo or card games
- Calendar
- Digitized pictures
- Plant meaningful to your history
- Flowers meaningful to your history
- Pedigree chart for framing
- Pedigree chart to add information
- Picture puzzle
- Family history quilt
- Paper dolls
- Family history website
- Timeline
- Workbook
- Anything related to your particular
  family history with a story
  and pictures about how it relates.

- Book about the history surrounding your family
- Book about your family history (picture book or full history)
- New scrapbook or scrapbooking supplies
- Instruction book and supplies for a family skill
- Digitized history such as journals or letters
- Completed oral history on video or transcribed
- Oral history questions and an appointment for an interview
- Hard copies of journals, letters, pictures
- Completed indexing or other organization project
- Family gingerbread house or family cookies
- Bags T-shirt, mug (like at http://zazzle.com) with a family crest or family saying
- Subscription to family history research website
- Tickets to a historical movie related to your history
- Registration for language, culture or hobby class
- Craft supplies to make a family history project together
- Tickets and arrangements for a family history trip
- Collection of tweets or blogposts about your family history

Other ideas that work with the youth in your family:

_____

_____

_____

_____

_____

_____

_____

_____

_____

_____

_____

_____

_____

_____

_____

Interview Questions

An oral history interview is a great way to learn about the history of your family. You can interview anyone, a close relative, a distant relative, or even a family friend. An oral history captures the subject's personality, their stories, their feelings, their hopes and dreams. Conducting an oral history interview catches the family's stories, their essence, the parts that aren't available later in regular documents.

What are the dates and any interesting stories surrounding your birthday and birthplace?

What are your marriage dates and divorce dates?

What education did you receive?

What homes did you live in?

Describe your father. What did he look like? What was his personality like?

Describe your father's parents.

Did your father have any siblings?

Describe your mother. What did she look like? What was her personality like?

Describe your mother's parents.

Did your mother have any siblings?

How did your parents meet?

What are some fun stories about your Mom and Dad? What was important to them?

How much education did your Mom and Dad have?

How would you describe your parent's relationship?

Describe your siblings. Where do they live? What do they look like? What are their personalities like?

What do you know about your family surname? Do you know its origin?

Are there any traditional first names, middle names, or nicknames in your family?

Are there any talents or interests that have been handed down?

Are there any recipes that have been handed down?

Do you know of any famous or infamous people in your family's past?

Are there any stories of great fortunes made in your family or lost? What were your family finances like?

Where there any common sayings or expressions in your family?

Are there any important people who have influenced you or your family?

Is there a family cemetery or burial plot?

What toys or hobbies did you like as a child?

Did you play with other children? Describe your childhood friends.

Describe your childhood home and yard. Describe your bedroom.

What was the area like around your home? Describe your neighbors or friends.

Did you have household chores as a child?

Describe your first school Who were your teachers?

Were there sad times or particularly happy times in your childhood?

Do you remember any little poems or songs from your childhood?

Did you cause your parents trouble? What rules did you have in your home?

Describe any birthdays you remember. How were holidays celebrated?

What was your family life like?

More Questions

What were your clothes like? What were your favorite clothes?

What childhood illnesses did you have?

What school did you go to during your teen years? Do you remember teachers?

Did you participate in any extra curricular activities?

Who were your friends in High School?

What did you do with your friends?

What interests or hobbies did you have?

What did you do during summer vacations?

What kind of grades did you get?

Who was the subject of your first crush?

How did you meet your spouse?

How did you meet your in-laws?

How did you get engaged?

How did your family feel about your engagement?

When were you married and where?

What parties or receptions did you have?

Describe your wedding day and honeymoon.

Where was your first home?

What kind of budget did you have to live on?

What were the first years of your married life like?

How did you find out you were going to have your children?

How did you pick your children's names and why?

What preparations did you make for the babies to come?

When and where were each of your children born?

What was your life like when the children first arrived?

What were some of the things you did with your children when they were young?

What traditions have been handed down in your family?

What was your family life like? What was the routine with the children?

What are some of the funny things your children did?

What was the nicest thing each of your children did?

What do you like about each of your children now?

Tell us about your parent's philosophy of raising children? How did yours differ?

What was your first job?

If you could do it all over again would you choose the same career?

Do you have any advice on finding a career?

Was your family religious?

What are some of your feelings about God?

Do you believe in life after death?

Have you had any major sicknesses?

More Questions

What are your greatest accomplishments?

Do you wish you had done anything differently?

What was the biggest turning point in your life?

What are you most proud of?

What are your dreams in your life? What are your fears?

What was your most embarrassing moment?

Have you been involved in any community or service activities or volunteer work?

Where do you stand with politics?

What personality traits do you admire and what traits have you tried to emulate?

Does your family have any heirlooms?

What are your favorites—flower, color, place, store, restaurant, season, book, song, movie, movie star, TV show, food, game or sport, hobbies.

Describe any pets you've had.

What types of music do you like?

Were there any major turning points in your life?

What have been your greatest joys?

What are your greatest sorrows?

What has been the most wonderful thing that ever happened to you?

What significant changes in technology have you seen in your lifetime?

What message would you like to leave to your descendants?

Other questions:

_____

_____

_____

_____

_____

_____

_____

_____

_____

_____

Suggestions for creating an oral history:

• Go through the list of questions and choose which ones to ask. Make sure you are diplomatic.

• Test the equipment beforehand.

• State your name, the place, the date, and the interviewer at the beginning of the interview.

• Don't interrupt. Have a pen and paper to jot down questions that come to mind so that you can ask them later.

• Make sure the interviewee is comfortable. Take breaks when necessary.

• Listen during silences. Let the interviewee collect their thoughts.

• Pictures, heirlooms and documents can be added to or talked about later.

• Refine and edit the interview later.

• You can't do it wrong. Don't wait. Just do it now.

Internet Sites for Kids

If you follow through all of the lists attached to the links below, you will have covered many quality resources on the web about involving youth with their family history. Here we've given you the best of the best to start with. We'll be adding new resources to http://www.zapthegrandmagap.com/resources as they come up so keep your eye on that website first for all the best ideas.

http://kids.familytreemagazine.com
Family Tree Magazine has built a brilliant website for kids about family history. They get kids so they made it fun, but they keep it on topic. With resources for teachers and parents, this is the place to start if you have a curious kid.

http://www.sesamestreet.org/parents/topicsandactivities/topics/diversity
Sesame Street has some great resources for younger children about diversity and different cultures. Look especially for Global Grover who can give young children a sense of geography and their place in the world.

http://disney.go.com/disneyvideos/animatedfilms/tiggermovie/tigerificfun.html
The Tigger Movie is a fun story for young kids about the lovable Disney character's search for his family. Online games and print activities are included on the website.

http://www.americangirl.com
American Girl is a fantastic resource for historical characters that girls can relate too. Their dolls and accessories are historically sound and their website has some fun historical activities too. Wonderful resource if they have a doll that matches the culture of your ancestry.

http://www.usscouts.org/usscouts/mb/mb056.asp
At US Scouts you can find all the requirements for getting the genealogy merit badge and the resources you need to complete it. The genealogy merit badge is a great way for scouts to get started finding out about your history.
http://meritbadge.org/wiki/index.php/Cub_Scout_Heritages
Likewise the Requirements for the Cub Scout Heritages Belt Loop and pin help prepare younger Cub Scouts for exploration on their family tree.

http://www.kakophone.com
Kakorama--One of the first things my kids were attracted to on the Family History Library's desktop was finding out what happened on the day they were born and who else was born on that day. A fun starting place.

http://spoonful.com/crafts/handprint-family-tree
http://spoonful.com/crafts/family-flag
http://spoonful.com/crafts/family-tree-magnet-set
http://spoonful.com/crafts/family-tree-ornaments
http://spoonful.com/crafts/family-photo-tree
Spoonful by Disney has several family history oriented crafts you can make with your kids. There is the handprint family tree, a family flag, a family tree magnet set, family tree ornaments, and a family photo tree. Take a look around and see what you can come up with to display your family's history.

http://www.ourstory.com
Our Story will let you create a timeline of your stories, pictures and videos. A video on the front page helps you get started collecting information and you can even publish a book once you have it all done.

http://www.enchantedlearning.com/crafts/familytree
Enchanted learning has a collection of crafts and paper templates for family history projects and journal pages.

http://familysearch.org/learn/wiki/en/Family_History_Activities_for_Children:_3-11
http://familysearch.org/learn/wiki/en/Family_History_Activities_for_Children:_12-%3F
The FamilySearch Wiki has a collection of fun links for children to learn about history, genealogy and their place in the world. Lots of games listed, especially watch for the mystery treasure hunt games for researching in the library in Salt Lake.

Search strategies for finding youthful family history resources:

Use parenthesis around phrases like "family history" or "personal history"

Follow the leads on good websites--they may lead you to other resources that you hadn't found yet.

Of course keep your eye on http://www.zapthegrandmagap.com and http://www.zapthegrandmagap.blogspot.com where we will bring you reviews and notices of other books and internet resources.

More Sites for Kids

https://familysearch.org/learn/wiki/en/Family_History_Activities_for_Youth
The whole Summer of Sleuthing Program produced by the Family History Library in Salt Lake is online and available for anyone to use. There are challenges created for different age levels and fun activities and forms to fill out the program.

http://familysearch.org/learn/wiki/en/images/o/o1/FS-branded-
=Telling_a_Family_Story.pdf
Family History Interview Form is a short group of questions you can print out and use when conducting an interview with a family member.

http://www.cyndislist.com/kids
Cyndislist has a great compilation of resources about youth and family history. Watch especially for the list of articles by Michael John Neill written for Ancestry.com Daily News.

http://www.byub.org/ancestors/
http://www.byub.org/ancestors/teachersguide/pdf/guide.pdf
The PBS Ancestors TV show has created a 61 page Teacher's Guide to help create lessons for youth that go with the show. It is a good step by step instruction for teaching about genealogy softened with great videos that you can purchase.

http://www.ngsgenealogy.org/cs/rubincam_youth_award/nomination_form
The National Genealogical Society's Rubincam Youth Award is given every year in two age groups to a student for writing a paper about their genealogy. The Senior category (grades 10-12) is awarded with $500, the NGS home study course a plaque and one year of membership to NGS.

http://www.devonfhs.org.uk/acornclub
The Acorn Club is currently the best site out there produced by a Family History Society for young people. The Devon Family History Society in Devonshire England supports after-school clubs and has put together a fantastic site to involve children on the web. Watch for continued resources on involving children in a school and club setting.

http://www.rootsweb.ancestry.com/~usgwkidz/

Many of the links at the volunteer site US GenWeb Kidz have expired but there is still a good list of Interview Questions for Kids and lists of old terms for careers and health issues.

http://www.rootsweb.ancestry.com/~cangwkid/

The Canadian GenWeb page for kids is the best of the GenWeb pages for children. There are a few links that are broken but most of them are still in good shape. If you have Canadian roots this is an especially good site.

http://www.rootsweb.ancestry.com/~census/kidz/
http://indexing.familysearch.org

Census Kidz is a USGenWeb site organized for children to be able to help transcribe a census. Along with the FamilySearch Indexing project, these are two great sites for kids to be able to start indexing records.

List other good sites that pertain to your family history here. Websites about your own family history are of course paramount to capturing your family's interest.

_____

_____

_____

_____

_____

_____

_____

_____

_____

_____

_____

_____

We'd love to hear about any great sites you find. Contribute any ideas to the conversation at http://www.zapthegrandmagap.com/submit.

Books

Some of these are out of print but I still list them here because you can often find used copies on Amazon.com or elsewhere on the internet. They'll all help you and the children in your family learn more about your family history together.

Beller, Susan Provost. *Roots for Kids*. Baltimore: Genealogical Publishing Co., Inc. 1989.

Boy Scouts of America. *Genealogy*. 2005.

Bruzzone, Catherine. *My Family Tree Book*. Kew: B Small Publishing. 2006.

Campbell, Starr Hailey. *The Adventures of James: A Trip to the Cemetery*. Anaheim: Creative Continuum. 2005.

Campbell, Starr Hailey. *The Adventures of James: A Trip to the Oncologist*. Anaheim: Creative Continuum. 2006.

Campbell, Starr Hailey. *The Adventures of James: Baby Sarah is Born*. Anaheim: Creative Continuum. 2005.

Campbell, Starr Hailey. *Youth in Family History*. Anaheim: Creative Continuum. 2005.

Chorzempa, Rosemary. *My Family Tree Workbook*. Dover Publications. 1982.

Clark, Linda. Penrose, JoAnn Rasband, Elise. *My Family History and ME*. Utah: Graphic Design Co. 1999.

Douglas, Ann. *The Family Tree Detective: Cracking the Case of Your Family's Story* 1999.

Frisch, Karen. *Creating Junior Genealogists: Tips and Activities for Family History Fun*. Canada: MyFamily, Inc. 2003.

Holik, Jennifer. *Branching Out: Genealogy for 1st - 3rd Grade Students*. Woodridge, IL. Generations. 2012.

Holik, Jennifer. *Branching Out: Genealogy for 4th – 8th Grade Students*. Woodridge, IL. Generations. 2012.

Holik, Jennifer. *Branching Out: Genealogy for High School Students*. Woodridge, IL. Generations. 2012.

Horowitz, Lois. *Dozens of Cousins*. Berkeley: Ten Speed Press. 1999.

Hubbs, Susan H. *Dig Up Your Roots and Find Your Branches: A Child's Guide to Genealogy*. Writer's Showcase Press. 2000.

Kalman, Bobbie. *Games from Long Ago*. New York: Crabtree Publishing Company. 1995.

Kenny, Karen Latchana. *Cool Family Parties*. Minneapolis: ABDO Publishing. 2012.

Koons, Bee Bartron. *Teaching Genealogy to Young People*. Westminister, MD: Heritage Books, Inc. 2004.

Leavitt, Caroline. *The Kids' Family Tree Book*. Sterling. 2007.

Leedy, Loreen. *Who's Who in My Family?* Holiday House. 1999.

Love, Ann. Drake, Jane. *Kids and Grandparents: An Activity Book*. Niagara Falls: Kids Can Press. 2000.

Matthews, Tony. *Memory Trees: family trees for the scrapbooker*. Baltimore: Genealogical Publishing Co. Inc. 2003.

Ransburg, Ashley B. *Evie Finds Her Family Tree*. Indianapolis: Indiana Historical Society Press. 2006.

Rice, George. *Toys and Games From Times Past: and still enjoyed today*. Nashville: Historical Folk Toys, 2004.

Shepherdson, Nancy. *Ancestor Hunt: Finding Your Family Online*. Children's Press. 2003.

Starkie, Jane. *Hw 2*t ur Fmly Hstry*. Bury: Family History Partnership. 2008.

Sweeney, Joan. *Me and My Family Tree*. New York: Crown Publishers, Inc. 1999.

Taylor, Maureen. *Through the Eyes of Your Ancestors: A Step-by-Step Guide to Uncovering Your Family's History*. Boston: Houghton Mifflin Company 1999.

The Book Studio. *Family History Kit*. New York: DK Publishing. 2007.

Unknown Author. *Hunting For Your Heritage*. Doylestown, PA:Discovery Comics. 2001.

Wolfman, Ira. *Do People Grow on Family Trees?* Genealogy for Kids and Other Beginners. Workman Publishing Company. 1991.

Wolfman, Ira. *Climbing Your Family Tree: Online and Off-Line Genealogy for Kids*. New York, Workman Publishing. 2002.

Yerkow, Lila Perl. *The Great Ancestor Hunt: The Fun of Finding Out Who You Are*. Sandpiper. 1990.

Zahn, Catherine. *All About My Family: Genealogy for Kindergarten through Third Grade Students*. Arlington, VA. National Genealogical Society. 1997.

Zahn, Catherine. *The Family News: A Teacher's Guide For Using Genealogy and Newspapers In the Classroom*. Arlington, VA.:National Genealogical Society. 2001.

Incentives

We won't call it bribery here. But sometimes when something is more your agenda then theirs, it doesn't hurt to have a little extra incentive involved. "Don't worry though. Many hard core genealogists will tell you that they became involved because their grandparent paid them to help with their family history efforts. Engaging the next generations may take a little prompting at first, but there are big pay offs for everyone involved in the end." from **Zap The Grandma Gap: Connect With Your Family By Connecting Them To Their Family History** *pg. 64.*

Try these:
Candy/Chocolate
Money
Favorite dinner
Special outing
Tickets to an event
Time alone with you
Television privileges
Sports equipment
Games
Books
Software apps
Movies
Party with friends
Free chore passes
Child chooses and activity
Trade Family History Dollars
for other treats and privileges.

Other ideas that work with the
hobbies and interests of my child:

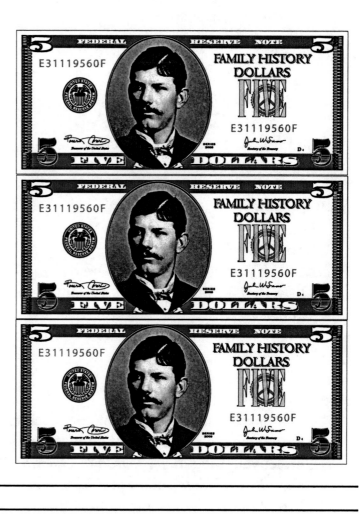

_____

_____

_____

_____

_____

_____

_____

_____

Starting Places

Here are some good starting places that are good for adults and kids who are interested in finding more information about their family.

Compiled Databases:
>   http://www.familysearch.org
>   http://www.ancestry.com
>   http://www.myheritage.com
>   http://findmypast.com

Popular Websites
>   http://findagrave.com
>   http://www.ellisisland.org
>   http://cyndislist.com
>   http://www.genealogybank.com
>   http://www.one-name.org

Standards and Hiring a Professional
>   http://www.bcgcertification.org
>   http://www.icapgen.org
>   Mills, Elizabeth Shown. *Evidence Explained: Citing History Sources from Artifacts to Cyberspace.* Baltimore: Genealogical Publishing Co., Inc. 2009.
>   Mills, Elizabeth Shown. *Evidence: Citation & Analysis for the Family Historian.* Baltimore: Genealogical Publishing Co., Inc. 1997.

Serendipity
>   http://ancestryinsider.blogspot.com/search/label/serendipity
>   http://thechartchick.blogspot.com/search/label/serendipity
>   Smolenyak, Megan. *In Search of Our Ancestors: 101 Inspiring Stories of Serendipity and Connection in Rediscovering Our Family History.* Holbrook, MA: Adams Media Corporation, 2000.
>   Jones, Henry Z Jr. *More Psychic Roots: Further Adventures in Serendipity & Intuition in Genealogy.* Baltimore: Genealogical Publishing Co., Inc. 1997.
>   Jones, Henry Z Jr. *Psychic Roots: Further Adventures in Serendipity & Intuition in Genealogy.* Baltimore: Genealogical Publishing Co., Inc. 1993.

Energize and Mobilize

The Plan

Now, let's make some plans. You know how important it is to share your heritage with your family members and especially the next generation of your family. So what are you going to do about it? Use these pages to put your goals into writing.

Easy and quick ideas:

Ancestor	Family Member(s)	Idea

More complex ideas:

Ancestor	Family Member(s)	Idea

Supplies	Specifics

Supplies	Specifics

We'd love to hear about your successes and what you learn about how to invest the next generation with their history.

Please send us an email,   janet@zapthegrandmagap.com
talk to us on the blog,   zapthegrandmagap.blogspot.com
tweet to us on twitter,   @zapgrandmagap
post to our wall on facebook   facebook.com/zapthegrandmagap
or submit your idea to share with others   www.zapthegrandmagap.com/submit.

Let us know how it goes. If you have an idea that sparks in your family and would like to share it with others, come join the conversation. Together we can figure out how to ground the next generation and send them into a healthy and strong future.

CPSIA information can be obtained
at www.ICGtesting.com
Printed in the USA
FFOW02n1718080117
31105FF